Creating Pop Culture

E. Naomi Omid

Published by EirianWrites Studios, 2024.

While every precaution has been taken in the preparation of this book, the publisher assumes no responsibility for errors or omissions, or for damages resulting from the use of the information contained herein.

CREATING POP CULTURE

First edition. February 29, 2024.

ISBN: 979-8223594079

Written by E. Naomi Omid.

Table of Contents

Dedicated to my parents, who taught me how to build
my world as a child.

And dedicated to Sam Stokes and Elise Thornback,
who taught me how to build my world as a grown up.

<u>**Chapter 0.0 – Introduction**</u>

This book is broken up into two parts with various sections within each chapter.

The first part of the book explains the history of Lazy Worldbuilding and the way that I have pieced it together over the years throughout my writing career.

The second part explains how to apply this method to your own work.

Feel free to thumb through this book, or to skip ahead to the "Creating Your Pop Culture" portion of the book, however, the best way to read this book is from beginning to end, so that way you can learn from the full 17+ year history of my world-building method and gain the most fleshed out road map to discovering your inner worlds.

<u>Chapter 0.1 - Prologue</u>

Back in 2021, I was just beginning to feel confident with my world-building technique, so I started quest writing for someone's author blog.

But, due to the unstable nature of the internet, the blog was defunct shortly thereafter and the original archives have been lost to the sands of time.

Yet, I never stopped thinking about how to breakdown my world-building shortcuts so that authors can play with urban settings and have as much fun as I have; because if I can save you 17 <u>years</u> of trying to figure out what "world-building" is and how to effortlessly apply it to your craft, gosh darn it, I'm going to.

So, flashfoward to 2024 and suddenly my alt-Earth, Th'aer, has 100's of books and several different series planned on it because it is such a vast and amazing world to live in. And now there is no denying that what I now call "Lazy Worldbuilding" needs to be shared with the writing community.

I have completely revised my original blog posts to reflect what I have learned since drafting them all those years ago, added the my own personal adventures of world-building, and have compiled it all here in this book for you so that you can write with ease and confidence while your imagination runs wild.

<u>Chapter 0.2 – What You'll Need</u>

Before we set out on our journey through the worlds I have created, you will need to pack a few things to bring with.

- *2 notebooks (one for notes, one for your story)*

- *a set of pens (I recommend having at least 2, one for each notebook, but you can never have enough pens)*

- *an "On-Off" switch for your Editor's Brain*

- *your imagination*

Now, if the third item down made you stop in your tracks because you have no idea where that switch is, don't worry! Believe it or not, I used to be the same way.

Your "Editor's Brain" isn't really a problem until you learn how to tap into it in the first place, which is really annoying because being able to go into "Editor Mode" is a really useful skill to have, but you do need to be able to turn it off before you can get any work done.

Think back to when you fell in love with writing.

When you were simply excited to get your story out of your head and hadn't thought about how the world would receive it because of COURSE it's good, it's YOUR book...

Sit with that memory for a few moments.

Breathe in the warm, childlike excitement of your determination and grit. Let that energy seep into your bones and light up your soul from the inside out... Then, begin writing in your preferred method (hand writing, typing, or dictation.)

This memory of discovering writing for the first time and the excitement that it creates is your "On-Off" switch.

It also helps to keep in mind that there will be several rounds of editing before you ever publish. The first go is always just the rough outline of your story anyways.

<u>Chapter 0.3 – Overcoming Writer's Block</u>

Writer's block is the absolute worst.

It is defeating and depressing, and is something I wish authors never had to experience.

Thankfully, once you've found the "On-Off" switch to your critical mind, you shouldn't really have writer;s block anymore. (It's really nice.) <u>But,</u> it does takes some practice to remove those mental obstacles for yourself.

In order to create pop culture in your craft, you have to be able to tap into a flow state where you turn your brain off, stop thinking, and just let the words pour from your being.

Personally, I have found that the best way for me to activate my flow state is to write with a pen and paper. It's not for everyone, but, I cannot imagine my craft without it.

"Hand writing" helps me stay in a free creative mindset, as though I am still 5 or 6 years old with no concept of "editing," because I know that this shaggy notebook is not what will be released into the world. It will have to be typed before it can even be edited, and, as an added bonus, the simple process of typing up what is in the notebook serves as a layer of editing in and of itself.

There is no word counter.

No red or blue squiggly lines to point out your errors, disctract you from writing, and turn your Editor's Brain on.

Just you, the pen, and the paper in an intricate dance as serene as fly fishing.

And it's something that can be done outside in the middle of the woods, or even by candlelight during a power outage if you wanted to.

The way the paper feels against the side of your hand as the pages fill with your visions is an absolutely one-of-a-kind experience, and somerhing I recommended that everyone tries.

And it doesn't have to be legible to anyone but you, either. It's like a journal entry. No one is going to read it, or try to decipher it, but you.

Outside of flow state, the number one culprit of writer's block is overthinking.

Regardless of how you do it while you write, you HAVE to stop thinking about the outline and just let your "pen" guide you at some point.

Once you can do that, the infinite worlds are your oyster.

Writer's block can also simply be a sign of imbalance somewhere else in your life.

Sometimes, writer's block is a sign that you are working <u>too hard</u>.

Take a break for a few days, or even weeks.

Go outside, get into a walking routine, or at least a <u>wellness</u> routine.

Meditate, take hot baths, use a sauna... Doing things that help to improve your circulation helps with your creativity overall, and self-care is the foundation for being a successful author.

You cannot properly share your art with the world if you are not taking care of <u>yourself</u> properly.

Other times, writer's block can be a sign of some kind of emotional or energetic drain in your life.

Whether it's eating too much bad food, partying too much, not getting enough sleep, putting up with bad or toxic relationships in your personal life, or even a social media addiction, anything and everything that takes from your energy without giving back to it also contributes to your inability to create.

If you find yourself struggling with writer's block, it may be time to stop and take inventory of your life and the ways that you spend your energy.

For me... it was social media.

After readjusting all of my other categories – eating better, sleeping more, prioritizing healthy personal relationships, and living the "soft life" nstead of gong hard at EDM Festivals, I still found that I didn't have very many ideas.

The thought of writing the <u>next</u> book seemed an impossible task. I could never have fathomed writing 20 or more!

But, as I stripped away my social media accounts – first Twitter, then Facebook, and finally Instagram – and reset my YouTube channel to be a platform for my books, more and more ideas started coming to me... to the point where now my joke with my friends is, "another day, another book idea."

It wasn't long after deleting my Facebook account and focusing my time on a personal blog instead of IG that I had my first series idea since 2019!!

And now, I have so many book ideas that I'm almost worried it's unrealstic... *almost.*

But it's a GREAT feeling.

RL Stein, famous children's and YA thriller author, has written and published over 300 books in his career and is still going strong... I think that my 100+ book goal is definitely doable.

At the end of the day, writer's block can seem like an insurmountable challenge that you will never be able to get around, but the truth of the matter is that the solutions are easier than you think, and writer's block will only stand in your way if you let it.

Take a step back and look at the big picture.

Maybe you just need to go out and live life for a few years (yes, I said "years") so that you have some experiences to write about.

Maybe you just need to reprioritize your focus.

And maybe... just maybe... you simply need to take a deep breath and write with wreckless abandon.

Part One:
The Lazy History of
Lazy Worldbuilding

Chapter 1.1 Exploring Uncharted Territories with Discovery Writing

The first time I ever plotted anything I was a junior in highschool, working on the first version of what is now <u>Finding New Haven</u>, which had undeniably been inspired by popular movies at the time... Particularly <u>Dawn of the Dead</u>, <u>Shaun of the Dead</u>, and <u>Zombieland</u>.

Actually, in that first version of <u>Finding New Haven</u>, Harley Monroe had gotten into a fight with one of her friends for taking "that zombie movie too seriously," menaing <u>Zombieland</u>.

Over time, the book completely morphed and changed into what it is now and scenes like that were completely cut out.

But, even in the beginning stages, my parents knew that I was taking this zombie book of mine far more seriously than anything else I had writte, and encouraged me to plot this one out.

Up until that point, I'd spent literally my whole life "just writing."

Sometimes I'd be able to tell a whole story, and sometimes I'd hit dead ends because I was exploring the depths of my characters' emotions but didn't have anywhere to go with the plot.

During that time, I found the most success with horror shorts because the backbone of the plot is already there, regardless of the finer details. (This is actually a method that you can apply to any genre fiction, and I highly recommend using it.)

Over the course of your career, you are bound to grow and change as a writer.

Certain tropes will no longer interest you if they are not true to the essence of your being. Your writing style will forever be advancing.

It is one of the most beautiful parts of being an author.

I spent a large amount of time writing horror.

Then, my life changed, and now I can only really write romance... and self-help (which is just another outlet for sharing love and good vibes!).

The nice thing is that, whatever you write, you can stay on the same planet if you would life... or, you can hop on your starship and move somewhere with a new vibe.

It is truly up to you!

I personally believe that every author should spend some time discovery writing, whether you publish those stories or not, and even though, eventually, you're going to need notes and outlines to keep everything organized.

When you're world-building, discovery writing is the author equivalent of hopping on your boat in the 1400's and sailing out to explore the <u>unknown</u>.

... How can you pre-plan the unkown?!

Well... you can't.

So, pick your characters and the conflict they're experiencing and just kind of drop yourself into the scene without having fully imagined the setting.

Then, just go with the flow – filling out the setting as the need arises.

The beauty of playing in a contempary landscape is that you're tasked with mirroring your surrounding and then adding your own flavor and perspective to them.

Eventually you will be the ambassador for the planet that you have discovered, needing to act as a trusted tour guide while you are also telling the story.

But, right now, there is a lot that <u>you</u> don't even know about your world yet.

There's an infinite amount of space for you and your pen to explore.

It's time to <u>discover</u>.

Chapter 1.2 – How I Stumbled into World-Building

As a kid, witches, wizards, vampires, and other such monsters wer my <u>jam</u>.

No joke, Halloween has been my favorite day of the year since the dawn of time, and I always, ALWAYS alternated between witch and vampire costumes once I was old enough to pick them out myself.

Other kids counted down the days to Christmas, or summer vacation, I was always looking forward to October 31st.

All time favorite songs include:

- *The Monster Mash*
- *The Purple People Eater*
- *They're Coming to Take Me Away, Ha-Haa!*
- *The Time Warp*
- *The Adaam's Family Theme Song*

<u>But</u>, I didn't start playing around with dark fiction until I was 12 years old, when I'd had a recurring dream about a vampire teacher...

Up until that point, I'd been writing fluffy stories with no conflict about girls living their dreams. (My favorite was one where a girl discovered she had a secret elevator in her closet that went to her very own, fully stocked, basement shopping mall. It was beautiful nonsense.)

<u>The Cry of a Midnight Songbird</u>, however, was about a junior in high school who was having an affair with her young English teacher, who turned out to be a vampire and wouldn't take "no" for an answer.

I love <u>The Cry of a Midnight Songbird</u> with all my heart, because it was truly the first novel that I wrote from beginning to end. But, this is actually the first time the concept has seen the light of day. I truly hope that I can find a way to re-purpose it in my paranormal romance series... just with a more appropriate age gap. Until then, it serves as a beautiful milestone in my long and arduous world-building journey.

<u>Chapter 1.3 – The Cry of a Midnight Songbird and the Birth of Lazy Worldbuilding</u>

It was early September 2006, I had just turned 12 that summer and had an intense crush on Taboo from the Black Eyed Peas, as well as Johnny Depp.

Pop culture was <u>all over</u> my rough draft.

And, thankfully, my parents did not balk at the subject matter. They did not tell me to stop writing such a dark novel. They did not restrain my creativity in any way.

They actually encouraged me to be <u>more</u> creative.

My parents didn't want me to rely on pop culture references in my writing for two reasons:

a. the references could become outdated
b. somewhere along the line it could potentially dip into the realms of copyright infringement

It turns out that the second reason isn't even really true. You can't use <u>song lyrics</u> or other intellectual property in your books without permission, but you can name drop as many brands as you see fit – that's actually a part of "contemporary" fiction.

But, I didn't know that when I was 12 years old, and thus, Lazy Worldbuilding was born.

I had already written half of the book when my dad gave me the challenge of replacing all the pop culture references with brands, actors, and store chains that I'd made up. And it was that process that had moved me from my home planet of Earth to an alt-world for the first time... even though I didn't really realize it in the moment.

<u>Chapter 1.4 – Destroying the World and Killing Zombies</u>

Looking back, all of my horror shorts also took place on the same planet as <u>The Cry of a Midnight Songbird</u>.

It was a black and red planet of shadows and blood. An entire world of death, misery, and revenge with no happy endings unless you were on the right side of the murder weapon and managed not to get caught. (My teen angst was quite a beast.)

But, I didn't really think about it that way until sitting down to put this together for you.

My horror shorts never mentioned pop culture like my novels.

Sometimes your planet is just a vibe.

At the time, mine was horror. (Like I said, black and red, blood and shadows.)

Sometimes that's all you need to write a story and work your magic.

The first rendition of <u>Finding New Haven</u> was the second time I specifically revisited the world.

Originally, Harley Monroe looted several different stores and found herself missing the hashbrown cakes from her favorite fast food restaurant, so I name dropped some of the places I had created for <u>The Cry of a Midnight Songbird</u>.

I hadn't realized at the time that I was burning "Horror Hollows" to the ground by introducing a widespread zombie pandemic, but it truly needed to be done.

<u>Finding New Haven</u> has gone through YEARS worth of editing to become what it is today; but the biggest piece to the puzzle was when my project manager, Sam Stokes, read an

earlier version and pointed out that she didn't understand the references I was making.

That life changing piece of input made me create a glossary for the world and forever solidified what I've been doing as a world-building "style."

<u>Chapter 1.5 – Exploring New Planets</u>

Per typical Lazy Worldbuilding fashion, I didn't realize that I needed a planet for the Faerie Lit series until I'd *written* the second book in the series.

The first book, <u>Did You Hear About the Prinz Party</u> was actually born out of writer's block. I'd written a Cinderella adaptation when I was completely blocked during my senior year of high school. Rewriting the classic seemed like it would be a good writing exercise. (And it was.)

But it wasn't until I'd lived a little and went to some music festivals that the story had life as a collection.

Like I said, I didn't even realize that I was writing in a new space. On a new planet.

Suddenly I was writing romantic fairy tales with happy endings, worlds away from the doom and gloom of my horror planet.

When I finally wrote the second book in the series, <u>Flashbacks & Afterglow</u>, was when I put the two and two together that this beautiful Faerie world couldn't exist in the same place as a zombie apocalypse, and separated the planets.

Admittedly, Th'aer <u>does</u> have some cross over brands because of this completely unplanned process, but, it adds a certain charm to the info in the back of the book and I wouldn't do anything differently.

<u>Chapter 2.1 – Building it Up</u>

Writing <u>Flashbacks & Afterglow</u> was a liberating experience.

It is the only book I've written where I only knew the characters and had no idea what the plot would be.

It's... pretty random.

But, I missed my "Snow White" character, Snowflake, who'd been the main character of the last short story in the previous book, and also had the shortest story in the collection.

What resulted is a beautiful, zany, patchwork story line that allowed me to fully settle Th'aer, once and for all.

PNK KanD even started out as a very small side character at the end of <u>Flashbacks & Afterglow</u>.

The book also helped to finalize the geography of the planet since <u>#SelfishSunday</u> takes place in a different town in the same state.

Story by story.

Piece by piece.

Bit by bit.

Th'aer started out as a lump of pink and blue clay that has slowly morphed and shaped into a fully evolved planet with a vast ecosystem of opportunities to explore.

<u>Chapter 2.2 – And the Rest is History</u>

Now that I know where I live and where my stories are set, I've started researching history and world-building new areas <u>before</u> beginning to write new stories there.

I loved sloppily, blindly exploring these new territories, but it's also really nice having a framework to build from.

Between the three series that helped to lay the planet's foundation, everything must now mesh and blend with what's already there.

Personally, I would never go back and completely change a story that I have already written and published.

I have uploaded fresh edits of a book, however, as that is one of the beauties of self-publishing your books. <u>Finding New Haven</u> hadn't truly been edited when I published it, so I had to hire an editor to help me polish what I'd written, so the version that is out now is almost twice as big as the original version, but I didn't *alter* reality, I only *added to it.*

As a result, every "About Th'aer" section at the back of each book has the same backbone, but then explains the Th'aerian information pertinent to the particular story. (Such as why Keoni Magnolia involuntarily time travels.)

Each glossary differs as well, only listing the Th'aerian terms mentioned in that specific book.

Now that I've begun working on <u>The Bargain Bush Chronicles</u>, a 69 book series of stand-alone novellas located in Wenstern Montaka, I have individual notebooks dedicated to character bios, the lore of various beasts and other phenomenon, as well as the history of the area in Montana this setting is based on.

And I am having the most fun writing I have ever had in my life!

Now let's breakdown Lazy Worldbuilding piece by piece so that you can harness this strategy without having to put seventeen years of trial and error into it.

Part Two
Creating Your
Pop Culture

Chapter 3.0 – Laying the Framework

Before you really begin and start blazing through your story, there are a few things you should prioritize first.

Now is the time to:

1. Define your genre
2. Define your map
3. Define your limits

<u>Step 1 – Define Your Genre</u>

Lazy Worldbuilding was designed specifically for Urban Science Fantasy.

It's a more contemporary adaptation of Science Fantasy, a genre that has actually been around for a long time.

Science Fantasy blurs the lines between science-fiction and fantasy, presenting a world with both magic and advanced tech.

Urban Science Fantasy puts those elements into the very familiar landscape of modern times.

The nice thing is, you can write whatever you want within the Urban Science Fantasy sphere. There is plenty of room for any story from horror to romance and everything in between. Urban Science Fantasy simply provides you with the setting for the stories you want to tell. It also helps give a reason to why you're world-building in the first place.

If you *weren't* writing Urban Science Fantasy, you'd just be writing contemporary fiction, which is great, but that's not why we're here!

Urban Science Fantasy allows you to add in magic, advanced technology, and paranormal phenomenon to take your storytelling to the next level; helping readers escape to a familiar place that is also more remarkable than the reality they currently live in. (And it's also, honestly, just a lot of fun.) It is the difference between a girl wistfully reminiscing about her ex-boyfriend, and her involuntarily time traveling into the past to be with him.

Life is mundane enough. Writing shouldn't be.

Go <u>wild!</u>

<u>Step 2 – Define Your Map</u>

As soon as you possibly can, design your map... even if it is just in your head.

With Lazy Worldbuilding, you'll likely be using some kind of version of your own town, state or country, but you certainly don't have to. You can go anywhere you want. You can create new lands if you see fit.

Just make sure to outline your territory borders and get some idea of the terrain. Is your setting a flat, grassy plain? A hilly city of skyscrapers erected during an industrial revolution era mining boom? An ocean town?

Having <u>some</u> sense of where you are inherently helps with the other finer details such as weather patterns, local climate, population density, access to resources, and so forth.

For <u>Finding New Haven</u>, I literally just based it in the US and, for world-building's sake, fictionalized the name of all the cities and towns mentioned throughout the book.

My new home-planet of Th'aer is a mirrored version of Earth.

From the name to the maps in the book, I'm not ashamed to admit that Th'aer is a little tacky. Quite the contrary. I am super proud of Th'aer.

I mean, come on now, this is <u>Lazy</u> Worldbuilding after all!

Th'aer has fairly sloppy beginnings from a world-building view point.

I am sure that any sci-fi or epic fantasy snobs would quickly sneer and pass judgment on what I've done here.

Like I said, this technique isn't for everyone, but it does help break down those barriers to genre accessibility. You can simultaneously create a new world *and* use your current modern surroundings. It is, quite frankly, an easy, quick solution for those who may be daunted at the task of Tolkein or Lucas style world building but want to weave tapestries with similar threads.

Th'aer was created, shaped, and molded because I was writing the <u>third</u> book on my home-planet and needed some geography, ASAP.

Yup, out of panicked necessity, I managed to slap together what is now my permanent home residence.

But, learn from my foibles, and don't be me.

Please, please don't be me...

Or do, I guess, because you ARE here to learn how to be <u>lazy!</u>

So, here's what I did to define the Th'aerian geography:

- I printed some maps...
- Flipped them over...
- And traced them.

Yup.

Sure did.

Knowing what I know now, I never would have done things that way.

In hindsight though, I also wouldn't do anything any differently.

It was a very real, raw, genuine moment and I am truly in love with the planet I live on.

Here are those maps by the way...

(*Maps by Keoni Magnolia courtesy of Blurtsberg High, Blurtsberg, Montaka)

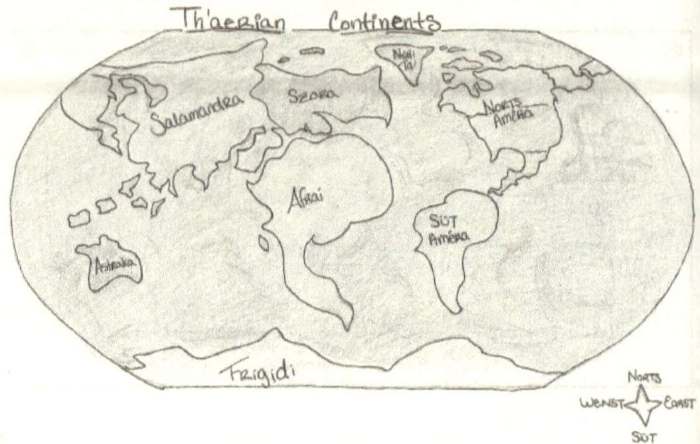
Th'aerian Continents
Salamandra
Szara
Nani Iai
Norts Amèra
Afrai
Süt Amèra
Astraka
Frigidi
Norts
Wenst
Eaast
Süt

Szonan Countries
Tutti
Cleveland
Joined Union
NORTS
WENST
EARST
SÜT
Marsupia
Marsupian Sea
Loka
NORTS PRRT
Schwitz
Finibora
Pokoko
Raklash
Beruj
UZimaS
Latvia
Bulgari
AYL
Fhtzen

Norts Améra Countries
Räkläsh
Nori Tal
Nori Mas
Utimas
Meraucia
Norts
Wenst
Earst
Süt
Süt Améra

UTIMAS
Nori Mas
HAYR
MONTON
NEW MAS
Masse Masse
DOVE AISLE
CROSCUS
NEW SWEATER
DEMI MAE
MARDOVA
New State
Vensberg
CHRISTOHN
HEOH
JEARST JEANINI
JEANNI
SPRUPI
NORTS ANGELA
SÜT ANGELA
NORTS
WENST EARST
SUT
FLORIKI
TÜNI BAMI
KESSE
TKORI
ROOTUS
ANA
DYANA
Royce
WISEN MAS
WOLOA
Hyota
NORI DAPRA
SUT DAPRA
NEMOTEP
KRAS
AKRAS OKIDO
TAPRAS
MONTAKA
ARIDI
TIRUDI
ÜTUS
New MERCUCIA
CAPO
WAYVE
Speesh
NAVIS
AZRA
CAPRICA
Mercucia
HAIKIKU
Nori Mas
ARTI MAS
ZAKKESH

I am still waiting to hear back from Blurtsberg High to get a copy of the Montaka state map with all the cities.

*See what I did there, to cover the fact that I am NOT a cartographer, and simply traced these maps and filled out the names, the story is that these maps were drawn by the main character in #SelfishSunday while she was in high school.

The reason why these were drawn by *Keoni* and not one of the other characters is because I didn't design the maps until I was writing #SelfishSunday. And also, she's the only character I had at the time with her high school years as a main part of her story.

And by the way, this "Through the Looking Glass" technique is by no means a new trick.

I am a comic book gal (if you couldn't tell.)

I mean I LOVE comics. Once one of my friends introduced me to comic books, I borrowed almost every series in her collection. I never buy comics for some reason... other people always have to give them to me, but, still to this day, when I need a break and want to read some fiction, I turn to the Scooby-Doo Apocalypse series rather than cracking open a novel. (By the way, if you like comics, Scooby-Doo and the apocalypse, definitely look up that series. It is PHENOMENAL.)

Comic books and animated TV shows employ this tactic a lot.

That's actually partially where I learned this trick and why I took on the challenge of renaming everything all those years ago.

All of my favorite series take place in some kind of alt-reality.

Batman being the best example.

Gotham is just New York City with a darker vibe.

So, live a little.

Stake a claim in your territory.

And draw some maps... even if it's just tracing over top of, or on the back of, where you already live.

<u>Step 3 – Define Your Limits</u>

The last thing you need to do before we begin is set some boundaries.

What things happen on your planet?

What things do not?

Is there any history that you need to keep in mind while you are exploring stories on your home-planet?

Take some time to consider the things that can and cannot happen in your world.

My personal journey was entirely hobbled together up until, like, 2022, so I didn't do these things all at once. For me, I wrote <u>Did You Hear About the Prinz Party</u> with hardly any magic at all, other than the fact that Cinderella's dress was gifted to her by her deceased mother. Then, I wrote <u>Flashbacks & Afterglow</u>, introducing a river mermaid based on Ariel from <u>The Little Mermaid</u>.

Next, I wrote <u>#SelfishSunday</u>, which is about a girl who accidentally time travels into the past to relive her 18th birthday, introducing the concept of time warps.

Finally, I began the PNK KanD Project which reveals that the Th'aerian entertainment industry is actually run by Fae.

And that's the point when I realized that I needed to put some structure behind this behemoth or it would start getting very inconsistent very quickly.

It started with a short explanation of the world's history, and a little poem explaining why Keoni experienced involuntary time travel:

<u>"Welcome to Th'aer</u>

A completely new planet

That seems like yours at first sight

But it's not just languages and countries
That have extra flair,
All sorts of creatures also live on Th'aer
In this particular book, we get to see
What seems to be some kind of time traveling
A unique event that can happen when
Magickal stars fall from the heavens

Life on Th'aer started in Afrai when wanderlust stricken mermaids crawled onto land and slowly adapted to being above water rather than under it. Afraiccians are characterized by their dark skin and coarse, curly hair. Afrai used to be in the center of the former mega content referred to as Terrona. However, Terrona has long since shifted and broken down into several pieces which drifted apart and remain as the Th'aerian continents known today. Th'aer has a long and complicated history of intercontinental violence and enslavement. The Afrai population in Utimas is largely due to the enslavement of the Afraiccians.

Afrai remains the center continent on the planet of Th'aer.

Life spread east, west, north, and south of what is now known as Afrai before Terrona separated in the Great Shifts. The separation of the lands created tribes of the same species with different languages, skin pigment, and cultural practices.

Today, Th'aer is very modern because of the magick at its foundation, and running through its veins as we speak. Other books on the same planet explore Th'aer's bizarre creatures which are intermingled in modern society, so I won't be going into any of those details now, because they were not mentioned within the pages of this tale.

However, the reason for Keoni's trip was the very special magick of a star falling through the night sky which caused a rift between all the nows to open up and sucked Keoni into the nows that she needed to relive to learn the lessons she needed to learn in order to mature into a higher being. This does not always happen when you see a shooting star, however, if that particular date is significant to the subject, and a loved one makes a heartfelt, passionate wish while a star falls, it is the typical chain of events." (#SelfishSunday, 2020)

Since then a lot more about Th'aer has been set in stone.

I ended up going with a vast and varied, galactic, magical and technological ecosystem.

Aliens travel to Th'aer and even immigrate there.

The cities harbor strong, electric type of crystal magic where the Fae thrive and have also founded the entire entertainment industry.

The rural, less densely populated areas harbor ancient, paranormal magic. It's where the werewolves, vampires, and other such creatures live.

And to tie it all together, humans still populate the vast majority of the planet. Some beings even grow up thinking they're humans, but they're really demi-gods or changelings (which is a really *beautiful* thing on my planet, not a scary one.)

But there are no zombies on Th'aer.

I draw the line at zombies.

So take a few minutes to figure out the things that are possible on your world and really lay down a structure for yourself.

Like I said, Th'aer has river mermaid witches with snake tails, but no zombies.

Setting those boundaries for yourself is super important so that you can always stay within reader expectations.

All of my readers <u>know</u> that if they want zombies, there's an entire series for them to explore that is <u>somewhere else</u>. And I'm sure any one reading a Th'aerian work would probably be appalled if there was suddenly *ZOMBIES* to worry about there.

In a later chapter, we will talk more specifically about magic systems.

Right now, you're just writing a shopping list of the elements your planet will need in order to thrive.

Free your mind and have fun with it!

It's <u>YOUR</u> planet.

What kind of things exist in your world?

Now that you've gathered those key bits of information, let's dive into exactly how to apply Lazy Worldbuilding to your stories!

<u>Chapter 3.1 – Real World Examples of Creating Pop Culture</u>

Creating Pop Culture is simply taking real world pop culture and putting your perspective on it.

It really is truly as easy as it sounds.

By definition, Creating Pop Culture means building a sci-fi or fantasy world with a focus on pop culture, similar to our modern world today.

A beautiful, real world, literary example of this is <u>ModelLand</u> by Tyra Banks, in which she was able to take her experience in the modeling industry and transform it into a fantasy story with an inspiring story-line throughout.

It's an incredible book.

Every woman/one should read it.

Storytelling is all about taking the reader or listener somewhere other than where they are in that moment, blurring the lines between what's real, and what's fictional.

What's strange, and what's familiar.

And, while some authors are able to take their pen and paint an entirely new world from scratch... I LOVE taking the world around me and stylizing it into something that is my own.

Contemporary fiction with a bit of an animated twist...

First off, think of your favorite cartoon. And if you're not a cartoon person, watch a couple of episodes of <u>The Simpsons</u> or <u>Futurama</u>. (<u>Futurama</u> is a much better example of this because it is in an Urban Science Fantasy realm.) If you haven't noticed, MOST cartoons have all their own brands, but they're still products that we know, creating an element of connection, since the strange world still has a thread of the familiar in it.

Another prime example of this is the <u>Grand Theft Auto</u> video-game franchise. Every car, store, radio station, strip club, tattoo parlor, and even the music played on the radio stations are all fictitious.

This tactic is employed in film and TV media to avoid copyright infringement, plain and simple.

And, like I said, that's why I did it too. I never realized that books have different rules.

I just knew that the only reason why your fave movies and TV shows get to mention your favorite brands is because they've been paid to.

I began creating my own pop culture simply by replacing all of my name drops. Cars, handbags, scrunchies, chips, whatever it may be, I can come up with a replacement name for the brand or product.

And then, one of my first editors mentioned how confusing and unnecessary it was... Unlike Sam, they just thought it took away from the story.

But...

It was a PART OF the story.

It's a huge part of my writing style.

That's when I fully formed Pop Culture Creation. Leaning into it HARD.

And now, I have unlocked another level of writing to play within. Not only that, but I've developed a method to the madness of replacing every single pop culture reference with a new concept. (That's why we're here!)

If you make it a point to really work at it and hone your skills, you will have a beautifully vast, rich world with endless possibilities, and infinite things to write about.

One of the brands you create could spark a spin-off series about the brand's originator and its importance to your world's culture. Or it could inspire a mundane-seeming yet totally magnificent quest for one of your side characters.

The possibilities truly are endless.

Pop Culture Creation is like putting two mirrors in front of each other, but in a tangible way. All because of the glossary you have to build to help your readers travel through your world. (That's really the secret: make things up, and then make a glossary so people don't get confused.)

But, once you get into it, there is a lot more that goes into this type of world building than people could ever imagine!

There's the back story, the look, the feel, the status... Pop Culture Creation also allows you to make connections from one character to another.

My favorite example of this, from something I've written, is that one of my side-characters in the Faerie Lit Series is revealed to be the founder of a clothing company in the PNK KanD Project. And I did so specifically because this character's name serves as a beautiful homonym for rap lyrics.

The PNK KanD Project is why Pop Culture Creation has become my author brand. Despite the fact that it's an urban fantasy and takes place on a planet with mermaids and faeries, my series is about a lady rappers and includes the lyrics and music to to with it.

And what do rappers write about most?

Their lifestyle.

The culture that I'm creating on my planet involves brand name drops and clever folklore.

But, when you're writing books, you must also create a rich history for your planet in order to provide an immersive experience and present a believable world.

You have officially been tasked with building a planet similar to our own, from the ground up.

You must pick the terrain. And you set the rules.

You write the history.

And once you have your characters, you must write your story. I recommend organically flowing, and then stopping to create a replacement when you come across something you want to mention.

Another fantastic example to close out with is the brilliant cinematic work of Kevin Smith.

His debut film, <u>Clerks,</u> takes place in a gas station, and thus, every cigarette poster, soda, and pack of gum is a "Smith Original Brand."

But Smith doesn't stop there. In the background of a far more recent movie, <u>Jay and Silent Bob Strike Back: Reboot</u>, Smith sneaks a poster spoofing his own title in the background of one of the scenes.

As authors, we get to take it a step further by explaining the jargon and the history behind it at the end of the journey. Building your glossary for the end of the book will also help you avoid info-dumping throughout the book itself.

I <u>highly</u> recommend keeping a list of everything that will need to go into your glossary as it comes up in your story so that way you don't have to go back and look for all the pop culture you've created.

To keep you in the flow of writing, it should just be briefly writing down a list in bullet point fashion while, jotting down your pop culture reference before diving back into the story.

Chapter 3.2 – Where to Begin Creating Your Pop Culture

So, it really is very simple.

Start your Pop Culture Creation anywhere you'd like. It's essentially an exercise in nouns. You're figuring out which people, places, and things have a place in your story.

Don't worry about the story behind the brand yet, just focus on the names for people, places, and things at first.

My favorite personal example of this is from <u>The Cry of a Midnight</u> Songbird. I needed a name for a teenage heart throb and unfortunately named him Luke Slobber, but at least he had a name. From there I branched out into stores, restaurants, fast food joints, and various types of musical artists.

Thankfully, these things change and grow over time. Sometimes you come up with a name writing the rough draft, and will have changed it four times by the final one. The first name you come up with is essentially a placeholder term. As you go back through during the editing process, you're going to come up with better, more stylistic names and terms. You might also catch yourself using too many synonyms in a row, or too many alliterations, which should be rectified in the editing process as well.

For example, if my heartthrob's name had been Luke Slobber and his co-starlet's name was Lucinda Squeaks, then I would have been told to change one of those names so that the LS motif doesn't get confusing.

You may also find that you change the name of something during editing, only to change it *back*. This happened with the doughnut shop in <u>Breakout</u>.

The placeholder name was D's Nutz, and after I changed it to something less tongue and cheek, I couldn't get the name "D's Nutz" out of my head. Now it has a lush and rich history that give life and meaning to the name, and I am overjoyed that I stuck with the original name.

On an unrelated note, your Main Character names can change too.

My main character in #SelfishSunday was originally named Anemone… and then someone commented on an Instagram post of mine that you couldn't pronounce the name drunk. Hence, the Keoni Magnolia series had formed. And in a salute to that historical fact, I named the pizzeria they go to towards the end of the book Anemone's in honor of that lost gem.

Start anywhere.

What or who do you need first?

A place to hang out?

A high value wrist watch?

The best place in town for a first date?

The song playing on the radio when your MCs leave on their first road trip?

What about the car they're driving?

Start there. Name it, claim it, prepare to rearrange it, and continue writing your story.

You can take it as far and wild as you want.

Later, you will need to think about the significance of the name mentioned, as well as the history behind it. You may even find yourself tightening up your degrees of separation and link more of the story than you initially anticipated.

For example:

Say that your main character carries around a laptop all the time.

If you have the history of the laptop, the main character could see the inventor speak at a convention, or meet them somehow later on in the series.

Also, make sure you don't leave a lot of unnecessary descriptions. Even if it's a red herring done intentionally, every description should have a purpose.

During the editing of <u>Breakout</u>, I realized that I had given in-depth descriptions for characters I had no intention of bringing into the story long term. In that case, you can either cut out those parts and add to the story in other places, or make note of it and leave it as a lead to come back around to you at some point later on in the series, developing an afterthought into a fully fleshed out character to interweave back into the story.

You need to know your main character, yes, and should have some kind idea for your story, true. But from there, the job of the rough draft is to help you find all the cardboard cutouts and props that you need in order to tell the story.

Trust the process. Things will flush out during the editing stage.

But, first, you have to have <u>something</u> that can be edited.

So, just... start writing.

<u>Chapter 4.1 – What Makes Life Familiar?</u>

We have this... coffee table that used to be *covered* in stickers.

We inherited it from our roommates almost a decade ago, and it serves as a piece of personal history as well as a testament to the things that make life go 'round.

At one point this table had beer labels, snowboard brands, store stickers, and even band memorabilia. Before my husband <u>finally</u> stripped the stickers off of it, I would still find things on the table I didn't notice before, or had forgotten about.

Pop Culture Creation is about creating new yet familiar experiences for your reader, so it's all about keeping the safety blanket of our modern world by your readers' side during the entire journey.

What stickers would be on your MC's coffee table?

Dirt bike logos?

A sticker for the local swimming pool?

Do they enjoy spending a lot of money on clothes, or do they prefer to dig all of their threads out of the bargain bin at the grocery store?

Also, what makes or planet familiar to you?

Take the time to sit down and journal some of your favorite childhood/ "pre-now" memories that really stick out in your mind, whether bad or good.

Take time to think about what makes your world go 'round.

What are the modern things on Earth that tickle you pink?

Where did you have your first date?

How did you celebrate your high school graduation?

Where was your first job?

As a writer, you get to take all of your life experiences and use them as research for the rest of forever!

For example:

My first job out of high school was at a gas station.

My first date in middle school was at the movie theater.

My favorite place to eat when I was in high school was the national chain with the cute cartoon redhead.

You can go into as much or as little minute detail as you see fit.

Although, I've found that it kind of snowballs as you write. First, you invent a cosmetics brand so you don't have to keep saying, "her magick lipstick," and the next think you know you're researching the history of toilet paper and cotton swabs because your main character wants to figure out a better make-up removal technique that is cost effective and won't damage the sensitive skin under her eyes!

Pop Culture Creation is a mirror, that takes you through your own looking glass.

So, before you begin this journey, take a step back and sit with the question: *What about this life do I have the most commentary on?*

That is the key to everything.

Because I've spent years in the "food" industry in the way of gas stations and grocery stores, those experiences, products, places, and industries have shown up in my writing in a big way. And because of Pop Culture Creation, I can take it as far and deep and long and hard as I want to!

And so can you.

Pop Culture Creation is like winning an exclusive tour of a chocolate factory where you find a literal forest of candy and soda that allow you to float in a gust of wind... your only limitations are your imagination.

Chapter 4.2 – Parodying versus Plagarism

I will never forget being 10 years old.

2004-2005 was a weird year.

Most notably, the book <u>Confessions of a Teenage Drama Queen</u> had been turned into a movie starring Lindsey Lohan, and it was my *everything*.

I saw it in theaters.

I bought the soundtrack.

And I played the music daily while waiting for the DVD to come out.

That was when I got my first lesson in parody.

You see, my father worked at the movie theater at the time, and one day he began singing his own lyrics to the song with the same name as the movie.

As a 10 year old, I was incredibly serious all the time and was phenomenally agitated by the event. These days, however, I can appreciate that moment for what it was – a pure moment of self expression.

With Pop Culture Creation, there is a delicate line between stealing ideas from the world around you, and parodying it. This line is one that you must define for yourself, and also separates mediocrity from greatness.

And then, once you define that line, you will find yourself dancing around freely in the space that you have created with reckless abandon.

Don't worry though, we all have to start out with the MacDenver's Hamburgers and Triple Fresh Mint gums. The truth is, you can't create a parody of anything without building onto someone else's ideas!

Pop Culture Creation is about fine tuning the process as you go so by the time it makes it to your readers, everything is 100% You, in your own authentic style, with your own personal flavor upon it. In fact, even if our planets are identical in THEME, there is no way we could possibly come up with the same worlds or products. Because I'm me, and you're you!

So, whether you've started writing already or you find yourself stuck and frustrated with this process, I want you to stop and take a break for a few days.

YES! For this writing course, I want you to stop writing and go watch some TV!

Yup! Go watch some TV!

Not everyone is lucky enough to have a zany parent who parodies song lyrics. So now it's time for you to do some homework so that you can appreciate the power of parody – because Lazy Worldbuilding doesn't work without at least a pinch of humor.

The TV show <u>Saturday Night Live</u> is likely the best example of this, considering they've been doing parody skits for decades. Although, I've always been more of an <u>All That</u> or <u>Amanda Show</u> type of person – which is probably why I lean into the fake products and commercials in my own craft so hard. My two favorite shows growing up included skits that were literally commercials advertising fake products like "Scream-in-a-Box."

<u>South Park</u> is great for research as well. Even though the show did not originate as a parody of life itself, however, they did adapt that approach when they realized how powerful of a platform they have. I am absolutely in love with <u>South Park</u>'s stunning and unapologetic social commentary.

But it doesn't stop at TV shows! We still need to discuss film!

Before we talk about parody movies, I want to briefly touch on "mock-u-mentaries."

Mock-u-mentaries are false documentaries, AKA, cinematic movies filmed in the style of a documentary, following the life or lives of fictional characters.

This is Spinal Tap, Behind the Mask, The Trailer Park Boys, and Parks and Recreation are all different types of mock-u-mentary movies and TV shows that I recommend watching in order to learn the art form of parody.

Now, most parody movies are blatantly known for "ripping off" ideas, because they take certain concepts and make fun of them. The one that started the modern parody revolution that we live in now was the Scary Movie franchise, which only makes sense when you know the movie they're parodying, but hey, test out your scary movie knowledge and have a laugh at some crass humor... you know, as a writing exercise. These days you can find a "fill in the blank" movie for any and every franchise. So you have plenty of options.

My favorites in that vein of the genre are: Spaceballs (an OG parody classic), Meet the Blacks (a beautiful parody of The Purge), Vampires Suck (for the Twilight naysayers in the room), and Disaster Movie (from when we thought the world was going to end 10 years ago. Ahh 2012, we were so naive!!)

The options are endless.

Chapter 4.3 – Creating Your Magic

Science Fantasy is an amazing genre to write in because it allows you to have advanced technology like space travel, without having to explain it scientifically like in "true" or "hard" Science Fiction.

You could even say that Science Fantasy is most akin to Space Opera, which is Science Fiction with a focus on people and relationship driven plot, but Science Fantasy adds in *magic*.

This magic can be as minimal or maximized as you see fit. It truly is all about what you want to write and the stories you want to tell on the planet you've created.

The big thing is that once you've laid down the grown rules, you must stay within them.

If there's something you suddenly want to do outside of the terms and conditions you've already set in place, simply build a new world and use new characters so that you can tell the story you want, without breaking your own rules.

And I'm not just talking about not putting zombies where they don't belong, either.

The rules of your magic, no matter how loose or firm they are, need to be respected.

If you break your own rules, you'll lose reader trust, plain and simple.

So, what are your rules?

What kind of magic does your planet contain?

Are your characters' powers genetic, needing to be honed through training, Harry Potter style?

Is the source an insect bite or some kind of traumatic yet survivable incident like a myriad of superhero comic book story-lines?

Maybe the source of the magic is one of your products – a soup that makes you invisible, or high heels that can stop time.

Speaking of which, what are the powers and supernatural phenomenon that your characters can utilize?

What do they have to defend themselves against?

Are the magical events ubiquitous, or are they isolated incidents?

Does everyone go through the same thing, or does everyone's experiences vary?

Here's how Th'aer's magic system works:

• The Magical Society makes up approximately 34% of the planet's population. The Magical Society being: Fae; faeries, mermaids, elves, sprites, and so on.

• The Paranormal Society makes up approximately 13% of the population. These are Werewolves, Witches, Vampires, Ghosts, also Demi-Gods.

• Humans with no access to magic at all comprise 45% of the planet's population.

• Interstellar immigrants make up 5% of the population.

• The remaining 3% of the population are mixed, either Starchildren (Human/Alien lineage), any kind of Fae/Human combination, or of mixed Witch/Human or Demi-God/Human heritage. (Demi-Gods are half-God/half-Human as well)

• The supernatural activity overall is ubiquitous and fairly random.

• It is regionally based. Paranormal Activity is mostly isolated to rural areas, where Magical Activity is more concentrated in the cities.

• The one rule that *is* set in stone is that *everything* is genetic. Not even <u>witches</u> are human on Th'aer.

Even though most of the beings living on the planet look like humans, humans are the only ones without access to any sort of supernatural pizzazz.

So, take some time to jot down a few notes about the magic system on your home-planet, making them as vague or as detailed as you feel.

This guide to your magic, no matter how brief it may be, is the number one tool that will make you a great ambassador to your world.

<u>Chapter 4.5 – Plotting versus "Pantsing"</u>

Every author has a different process for writing a book.

Some books are long. Some short.

Some authors craft an entire story in just a few hundred words.

But, regardless of your preferred story length, there will always be a debate on whether you should plot your entire story, or if you can get by "Pantsing," or writing the story with no plan.

And there is no right answer to how to write your story.

Throughout my career, I have tried both methods.

I had an incredibly detailed outline for <u>The Cry of a Midnight Songbird</u> because it had come to me in a dream, but I never wrote it down anywhere, and I wasn't entirely sure how it would end...

Because of this, I never really *finished* the story in its entirety. I left it on a cliffhanger and could never continue on.

<u>Finding New Haven</u> had an entire cork board covered in sticky notes dedicated to it.

I had a plan and lots of minor details worked out.

But, in the grand scheme of things, a *lot* of those details got cut out and reworked and revamped over the years, and *years* of editing and revising I did on that story.

And, honestly, I think that the grueling outlining process is what gave me writer's block in the first place.

I thought that I would never write another book again.

It is important to try *both* methods, even though some "experts" may say that outlining is the only way to go.

"Pantsing" allows you to just be free in the moment, discovering the story as it comes to you.

The first time I tried this was with <u>Flashbacks & Afterglow.</u> It was very refreshing.

Of course, at some point, I started having an idea of the story that I was telling, especially because the Faerie Lit Series requires me to weave in a thread of some preexisting fairy tale. But at the beginning, I had *no idea* what was going to happen in that book.

Personally, I think that creating your World Guide is more important than outlining your story, but, both serve their purpose.

Having a World Guide allows you to "Pants" a book with more ease, because you know the world that you are playing in.

Outlining is particularly useful for long running series, and for juggling multiple projects at once. My best friend, Elise Thornback, taught me that writing your ideas down allows you to capture them so that you don't forget them by the time you can actually write the story.

Once she gave me that precious nugget of information, I have never looked back.

The PNK KanD Project is my most thoroughly plotted out serious, because of how intense it is. <u>Behind Closed Doors</u>, the sequel to <u>#SelfishSunday,</u> is also heavily plotted out because it needs to be.

These days, even if I choose to "Pants" a story or series, I have *some* idea of the plot.

The Faerie Lit Series is the best example from my bibliography, because they're retellings of stories that have already been written. As long as I know the rules of the magic around me and know the topic of the book, I can write fairly freely.

The biggest thing is to have well fleshed out characters.

Whether you do this in editing or in your "Pre-Writing Stage," your characters need to be realistic. Readers will not put up with cardboard cut out characters for very long.

So, whether you plot or "pants," just make sure that you know who you're writing about, and everything will be just fine.

<u>Chapter 5.1 – Creating Clothing Brands</u>

Now that we've discussed the fundamentals of what, where, why, and how, it is time to talk more specifically about creating believable brands.

This chapter is all about creating believable clothing brands and fleshing out what they mean to you.

Fashion is one of the key points that pop culture centers around. Not only that, but clothing serves as a way to separate classes of people, as well as to show off your political and environmental stances. — And that's before ever touching on your character's style!

Take the time to think about what people on your planet are wearing.

Is there a social caste system where the royals or politicians are dressed to the nines while the general population is forced to craft their own clothes out of hides and fabric scraps – a la <u>Hunger Games </u>style? Are things on your planet a bit more neutral? Or does everyone wear the exact same thing?

Where do people go shopping on your planet?

Do they go to a store front or do clothes materialize in the closet?

How are clothes on your planet manufactured?

Think about it.

Like, really, truly think about it and write down all of your answers in your Lazy Worldbuilding notebook.

How does fashion *affect* your planet?

Currently, on our real-world planet, we are seeing this sustainability "war" where you can choose to buy a whole new wardrobe for $10 every single week, or you can choose to invest in your closet so that you know your wardrobe wasn't poorly sourced by spending large sums of money... OR you can land yourself somewhere in between and stay sustainable and budget friendly by shopping at the thrift stores (which is my favorite option.)

When you are creating pop culture, all of these things have the possibility of coming up — even if you, as the author, are not a fashion forward human in your own life.

What about at school?

Did you ever wear a school uniform?

I did not grow up going to a school that required uniforms (outside of gym class). However, I was able to appreciate the fact that I didn't have to, because clothing is a form of self-expression. I also loved books where the main character was frustrated because all they wanted to do was express who they really were, while the mandated school uniforms would not allow it.

The clothes one wears is the equivalent to the paint on a house and the landscaping in its yard. They tell you whom you are approaching, and can even deceive you if a high class person is "slumming it", or a vagabond has gotten a luxury makeover.

Before they get to know who you really are, clothes are the cover that people judge your spiritual book by; or, in the instance of uniforms, allow people to judge your soul and your actions instead of getting distracted by your adornments.

Wardrobe choices also serve to oppress or display the cultures of the people on your planet.

Most dystopian sci-fi novels I've read present the idea of a unified code of attire —grey jumpsuits, for example — to help diminish the idea of individuality and is often the cause of inner turmoil for the MC, who daydreams of an escape to a freed existence.

There's plenty of ways to spin this, but, unless your planet is entirely populated by nudists, you will eventually need to touch on the attire of your people. You could even take it one step further, and define different styles of dress for different cultures across your planet.

So, where do you even begin?

The first step is always going to be defining your planet, your people, and your story. After that, you can decide what kind of brands exist on your planet, their significance to the population, and the story behind them.

In my own work, I name drop a LOT of brands, and they're consistent across the board. For example, if FlooZ Wear was a high-profile, highly desired brand on my planet that only elite celebrities wear; I would use FlooZ Wear as a status symbol for my celebrity MC's as well as mention it as a highly desirable brand in a sister-series about common-folk on the same planet.

But, it doesn't stop at who wants to wear the brand and who can actually afford it. Creating realistic pop culture includes thinking about signature designs, materials used, products in the catalog, and the company's history, even business practices if you want it to. (It might sound like a lot right now, but just focus on the basics. We'll talk about company histories at the very end when we discuss building your glossary.)

In the example of FlooZ Wear, the questions to answer would look like this

- Who wears the brand?
- Who is the brand marketed to?
- Do they have a more affordable "ready to wear" line?
- Do they market to all genders or just one or the other?
- Have they always been a high class brand?
- What do they specialize in? Leather and fur? High-quality organic fiber? Shoes? Timepieces?
- How long have they existed?
- What does the brand signify to the main character?

• What are the signature looks or pieces that the company produces?

The list can go on and on.

In fact, as you answer these questions, you may find more questions keep popping up in your brain to help elaborate on these key ideas and transform your two dimensional words into a nearly tangible product line that your readers will wish existed.

And remember: no one starts out an expert! As you build your brands, you WILL need to research.

If you are creating a luxury clothing brand, you will need to know what that means — how luxury fashion houses operate, proper terminology, what separates luxury from bargain designed...

Pop Culture Creation is all about shaping a believable world and urban culture. You simply cannot mad things up as you go and call it a day. What is going to separate you from beginner world builders is your willingness to take new information so that you can present a well-rounded experience for your readers that has a level of depth they never expected possible.

<u>Chapter 5.2 – Fast Cars and Goin' Far</u>

Every planet that has undergone some sort of industrial revolution requires transportation. One of the greatest marvels of our society, in my opinion, is human travel. I mean, we've figured out short term/distance time travel, and I just think that's absolutely amazing.

So, whether you're working with trains, planes, automobiles, spacecrafts, or horse drawn buggies, you need to know how your people travel, and also how they would trade goods long distance, even if you never share that information with your readers.

Depending on whether you are a seasoned author with loads of titles under your belt or just starting out on your professional writing journey, this might have never even crossed your mind before! But, never fret, it's okay. In all honesty, being an author will always be a work in progress. The more you write, the more your craft will change and grow. Things that you never considered when you started this journey may pop up later on that seem shockingly crucial to the world you are building or the plot you've been working on.

I started designing fictional cars the instant I began my creating my own pop culture. It's in my blood. I've always been a car gal. I just love the sleek lines of sports cars, the history of car racing, and going fast in a status symbol. In fact, the one thing that *did* tie my horror shorts into the same world as <u>The Cry of a Midnight Songbird</u> was the cars.

But it wasn't until I met Elise Thornback in 2019 that I began taking my world-building seriously and looking at my world with a microscope to figure out the inner workings of it all.

It takes time.

Especially because you can't just say the name of a fictional car like nothing has happened and call it a day (trust me, I've tried. Sam called me out on it!)

You must know what the significance of each vehicle mentioned is. Also, keep in mind, the more you mention your signature car, the more likely your readers are to instantly know what you are talking about. Eventually, you will need to keep some kind of World Guide so that you can remain consistent in your story-lines and series' across your planet or galaxy.

Like with the other things you have been designing for your world, the questions you will want to ask yourself include:

Is the vehicle a status symbol?

What status does it symbolize?

What is the shape of the vehicle?

What are the lines it has?

How about the headlights? What shape are they? How bright?

What does the car's logo look like? The paint job?

Is it straight off the lot? Custom?

Chipping with rust spots showing through?

What color is the car?

What purpose does it serve? Is it safe? Practical? ...Dangerous?

How does it run?

Is the car "cherry"? Does it run like a top? Or is it constantly a point of stress for your main character?

Do they have this awesome looking car that barely runs and always needs work?

Does your MC spend more time walking and taking public transit than they do in the vehicle they actually own?

Furthermore, what is the importance of the vehicle?

Is it an homage to good times now gone, deteriorating in an overgrown field? A stationary chill spot in your MC's driveway? Does the car only come out of the garage for special occasions?

Art imitates life.

It also creates life.

That's what we're doing here, creating a new existence for your readers to get lost in.

Maybe your Main Character works on a factory line manufacturing cars too expensive for them to afford. Maybe they live in their car because they are an aspiring comic with no desires to be tied down to traditional living. Or maybe they are involved in a car accident which changes their lives forever.

It's all in your hands.

Another point of consideration is the size of the vehicle.

Are you writing about a beat-up SUV or a luxury two-door? Perhaps your MC is driving the single person car of the future...

Or maybe your character prefers motorbikes.

Then, when it comes to other means of transportation, such as planes, trains, and busses, what level of luxury is your character sitting in?

Are they cramped and feeling trapped on a charter bus full of odd and foul smells, with no leg room to speak of?

Do they have a private cabin on a luxury commercial jet? How much did their ticket cost?

How is it relevant to your story?

It doesn't make sense to add in these transport vessels if it's just filler or part of a step-by-step checklist; everything that you put in your story needs to be *pertinent* to the story.

Sounds obvious, but I wouldn't even be saying something if I hadn't heard the exact same thing from my editor.

Personally, I like to use travel for those self-reflective moments. Some inner dialogue, or perhaps, important relational bonding.

Because every little detail needs to have meaning.

It's the same principle as not showing a gun in the first act of a play if you're not going to use it in the third.

So, what are the main characters on your planet driving, and why?

It's a question that only you can answer.

Guess you better get started.

<u>Chapter 5.3 – Creating Your Entertainment Industry</u>

I will never understand why, but I have always loved the entertainment industry. Even when I was too young to understand that entertainment is its own industry, I was *fascinated*. But, it wasn't until I sat down to write this that I had truly contemplated the depth and origins of it all.

On Earth, "entertainment" has been around since humans really evolved into... humans. But, if you take a look around, you will notice that <u>every</u> species "entertains" itself, because without some kind of way to pass the time, this existence would become very monotonous for us ALL. And humans happen to be really good at storytelling. It's how we've had to share the things we've learned as a species since day one.

From cave drawings and interpretive dance to spoken and written word to music and painting on canvas, it's all just... stories.

So, in my humble opinion, art and entertainment should be woven into your world's culture as it is an ancient cornerstone within our own evolution. Thankfully, that can take shape in an infinite amount of ways on your planet, simply adding a bit more clay to your inventory!

With my work specifically, I use the entertainment industry to be able to name drop fictional musicians, hold concerts, go to movies, and so on.

Pop Culture Creation is truly an ode to youth culture and the bubble-gummin' activities that come with that particular Petri-dish.

Think back to what mattered to you as a teenager – impressing friends, fitting in (or standing way TF out), wearing the right clothes, and keeping up with the times.

Even as an artsy loaner, I worried about all of those things, so whether subconsciously or not, you probably did too.

What message do you want to send to those people who need you to be able to cut through all of that nonsense so they'll hear you?

That's what your fictional entertainment industry is for — being able to cut through all the fluff to send out your message subtly and distinctly.

This can look like writing from the perspective of a celebrity or simply having an underground house party... or even just taking your MCs to an art museum.

Entertainment shapes who we are. The stories we absorb change us as human beings throughout the course of our entire lives. And in a modern civilization with such a thing, who we make celebrities and give our time to is super important.

My favorite example of this in fiction is ModelLand by Tyra Banks, which I also mentioned in an earlier chapter of this book. ModelLand is about an entire fashion industry civilization and delicately dissects the harsh nature of the industry in a wildly, beautiful fantasy setting that took years for Tyra to compose.

She turned an entire industry into a civilization/planet and put it under a microscope with a psychedelic, kaleidoscopic lens on it, because she'd observed things in the world around her that she felt compelled to take a stance on.

So, take a step back and take a better look at what entertains you.

It may sound silly because you know what you like, because you like it, but grab a notebook and write down all the forms of entertainment that are important to you.

Video games? Movies? Magazines? TV shows? Board games? News? Radio? Books? Fiction or Non?

Other than writing, how do you fill your time?

Now, which of these also applies to your current main characters?

Even if it never comes up in the story, spend some time thinking about it and writing it all down because knowing these things about your characters will help you build better, more believable experiences in the long run.

You never know what might happen.

<u>Chapter 5.4 – Popular Technology</u>

Technology is another one of those things in society that completely shapes it, without us thinking much about it. By definition, technology includes everything around you. So, even though "technology" may feel very limiting, it is quite the contrary. What set out to be a chapter about making up your own computers and smartphone apps, ended up being an ode to creativity and original thought. So, strap in, because this chapter may take you by surprise.

The New Oxford American Dictionary defines technology as, "the scientific knowledge for practical purposes, especially in industry."

That's it.

That beautifully vague and fairly simple definition helps to throw the doors of possibility wide open.

"Technology" is not limited to computer sciences, it is everything that makes your society function on a highly evolved level.

Whether it is a post apocalyptic shower made from pulleys and a tin-can, or a supercomputer that can fit in your hand, it ALL counts as technology. Even in the fantasy world, you could change the words "scientific knowledge" to "magical knowledge", and then, away you go! The possibilities are endless.

When it comes to Pop Culture Creation, the theme is mimicking modern day, human life. And since the "Pop" in "Pop Culture" simply stands for "popular", there really are infinite options for you to create because *you* decide what is popular on your planet.

Technology isn't just what digitally connects the modern world. Technology is more over the broad spectrum of things that help society to function.

Technology is science (or magic) put into action to help make things work more efficiently. The first Being to attach a round stone to a wooden cart made an advancement in technology, helping homo-sapiens continue to evolve. Life is not without technology — even in nature. The nests that ants, birds, and bees make are all examples of natural technology.

As an author and curator of Pop Fiction, it is your job to decide how much modern technology your planet uses, what purpose that tech serve, and what the history is behind it — no pressure.

Are your characters fully plugged into digital reality?

Are they diligently working to create a world that will be?

Or perhaps yours is a postmodern planet, left with no power and only the anecdotes from the wise ones to serve as the proof that the little black mirrors in their pockets used to light up with magic and infinite wells of knowledge.

In our computer tech based modern lives, it is easy to forget that using a knife to cut food is also technology. Creating a torch for light, a hut for shelter, and a fire for warmth are also all displays of technological advancement.

So, take a step back and remember how broad the "technology spectrum" really is.

Yes, technology is cellphones and digital space; it is also telescopes and deep space rocket ships; but before all that, it was papyrus and charcoal.

Before your people were fighting intergalactic battles, they learned how to get to space; and before they were in space, they had to learn how to fly inside the atmosphere... and before they could learn to fly, they had to wonder if it was possible in the first place, and be determined to figure it out. "Technology" is the one thing we use CONSTANTLY throughout our day to day lives that we pay no mind to. Very rarely do you pour a cup of coffee and think —- *"Wow, someone learned that heat and clay equals a hard object and then figured out waterproofing methods and now mugs are a thing. Technology is great!"*

There is no, *"It's amazing that I can sleep on a mass-produced bed!"*

No, *"Science made it possible for me to recline with a footrest while sitting on my favorite couch!"*

Seriously though... when was the last time you thought about life like that??? (Never? Oh good, me neither!!)

With world building, it's not about letting your MCs acquire smartphones 10,000 times more powerful than what we have access to, it's about pressing pause, zooming out, and figuring out how all of the pieces that make this picture complete, came into existence in the first place.

It's time to take a moment to truly learn and understand the logistics of how your world functions.

And I mean EVERYTHING.

Like, down to the construction materials.

For example:

• Is flooring mass manufactured or does every carpet need to be woven by hand?

• Is food mass distributed or do you need to be on your neighbor's good side to get a healthy amount of veggies?

• What is the commerce on your planet like? Do your people trade equal valued time and goods for goods and services, or are they stuck receiving paper tokens for time and trading those tokens for goods and services?

• Did things used to be different or has this "always" been the way things were done?

I think that, as authors, it can be really easy to get stuck in the things we already know (I mean, hey, I built a brand off it, but that's not the only way to go.) Because, as authors, we've always been the weirdos.

The odd ducks.

The lone wolves.

And deep, deep down, every ugly duckling just wants to be accepted as the beautiful swan they are. So, on varying levels, we all want to fit in. (Don't worry, your secret is mine, and I ain't tellin'!)

The real beauty comes when you embrace the fact that you are a swan and *not* a duck!

You've got to dig deep, take risks, and write about what really inspires and motivates you. Don't worry about what everyone else is writing about!

Yes, it is good to take classes, research marketing strategies, and learn new skills, but don't think that just because someone else is writing a very similar topic that yours is somehow lesser than. You are a divining rod for the universe. It is only an injustice to your divine work to not share the stories and visions given to YOU!

Just because everyone else writes fiction with tons of computer science involved doesn't mean that your story about humans without computers isn't any less important.

And I say this lovingly, because I've been through this. ... twice.

In 2020 when the pandemic hit, there was an explosion of pandemic themed fiction.

It was quite impressive how inspired people were by the event.

I, on the other hand, had to completely vault the dystopian sci-fi series that I was working on at the time, and take a break from my zombie series because shit was too real — and that's okay.

The other example I have is with my Cinderella retelling.

There are hundreds, if not thousands of remodels of the Cinderella tale.

And, ironically, there is even a new sub-genre of horror fairy tales which is a genre (meaning horror) that I had to get out of about 10 years ago for mental health reasons.

My Cinderellas are about trauma recovery and breaking generational curses.

All versions of Cinderella are equally important, and mine being so wildly unique doesn't make mine any less important than the thousands of other Cinderellas.

Work your magic.

Analyze the places in which "scientific knowledge" is utilized "for practical purposes, especially in industry," and allow yourself to be as limitless as that statement.

<u>Chapter 5.5 – Good Eats</u>

The type of food references you make will entirely depend on the story you tell, and what matters to your MC.

If they eat a lot of fast food and prepackaged morsels, you may find yourself mostly focused on brands and franchises. But, if your MC is more of a health nut, natural foods like berries, fruits, veggies, fish, and teas may be your starting point.

The fun thing about food is that it impacts how your characters feel, and even tells your readers about who they are. Since food connects the human experience as a basic need for survival, it is a great way to connect with your readers.

I like to use restaurant and fast food chains in my work because they serve as a setting.

And there's always so much to take into consideration when it comes to food.

How does it taste? Smell? Feel? ... *Sound?*

What is it made of?

Are the ingredients natural or artificial?

Is it nutritious?

Why do your characters enjoy eating it? Or not?

The food in your book should not just "be there." It's not just a packaging or a store front, it needs to have a reason for being there, and should be an *experience* for your readers.

Bon Appétit!

<u>Chapter 6.0 – Putting it All Together</u>

Putting it all together is really as easy as it sounds once you have all the pieces to your puzzle. The hardest part is avoiding the temptation to info dump into the story.

You have to leave just enough context clues so your reader knows what you're talking about, without pulling them out of the story.

Building your own planet is a lot of fun because it allows you to write an infinite amount of books with a seemingly infinite amount of characters.

Not only that, but it allows you to slowly reveal glimpses of what you know, without having to explain the whole whole world to your readers all at once.

That's why it's important to know your limits, define your maps, and understand your magic system before you really dive into writing stories. Having the information for yourself allows you to pin point exactly when and where your reader will need to know the things you do.

<u>Chapter 6.1 – Creating Your Glossary</u>

Your glossary is where you get to divulge the secrets that you had to withhold during the actual story.

And, you can go as in depth as you want, or not.

The thing about a glossary is that some people might not care enough to read it. (But honestly those people are missing out!)

I always keep this in mind when writing, and take the most inspiration from the book <u>Watership Down</u>, which has to explain an entire rabbit language at the end of the book.

With your glossary, even though you are stating the facts, you still need to be engaging so that your readers will <u>want</u> to peruse the entire glossary.

Here's an excerpt from the glossary in <u>Breakout</u> because it's my favorite glossary so far.

- **<u>Chub Thug:</u>** Cleveland Butterfield, better known by his stage name Chun Thug, and later his alias Cleatus Clove, was a Utician rapper located in New State City. Considered one of the most influential rappers in the history of the genre, Butterfield is among the best selling music artists, having sold 80 million copies world wide. An innovator of lyrics, Butterfield would pour storytelling and traditional poetry into his bars. His goal with his music was to bring awareness to the inner city turmoil - very similar to the turmoil experienced in D-block, hence why he was one of John-John's favorites. Born May 3rd 1971 and shit in a gang related drive-by in 1996, ironically the same week as John-John's death.

• **<u>Cosmology:</u>** the main religion on Th'aer, similar to Earth's "Christianity", yet centering around the Cosmic Daughter rather than the Heavenly Son.

• **<u>Cosmic Daughter:</u>** Th'aerian religious deity, also known by her mortal name – Selene.

• **<u>Skipman:</u>** personal portable cassette player.

• **<u>Royal C.R.N.N:</u>** Trenton Lamar, better known by his stage name Royal C.R.N.N, Royal T, or simply C.R.N.N (crown), was a Utician rapper, also located in NSC, and deeply rooted in the origins of gangster rap. Lamar is so known for his lyrics outlining the criminal activity of his branch of the Goblins, it's a wonder he never went to jail for it. Lamar was also known for reinventing the lady rapper persona by bringing his side chick - Evelyn Banks - into the music industry and encouraging her to magnify that image. Born in 1972, Lamar only lived to the age of 24, having died in a drive-by shooting in 1997, which was undoubtedly retaliation to the shooting of Cleveland Butterfield. Despite the gang activity, Lamar remains one of the most respected and studied rappers in history.

• **<u>Lady GodDiva:</u>** Lisa Arnette Godson is a Utician rapper, singer, songwriter, and record producer. Her music career began in 1991 when then R&B group - Goddess Grove - debuted their first album. In 1993, Godson joined the Funk Initiative. She began her solo career as Lady GodDiva in 1997. Her premiere album, The Flyest Butter, debuted at number 3 on the StreetSign 200, the highest charting debut for a lady rapper at the time. Godson went on to produce a new studio album every other year until 2005, at which point she was diagnosed with an immune disorder and was forced to turn focus to her health.

• **<u>StreetSign</u>:** a weekly music and entertainment magazine known for its accumulative list of the most popular music every week - taking into account both radio plays and record sales, up until 2008 when they changed their routine to include online streams as well.

• **<u>Petite Miss</u>:** Evelyn Banks, more commonly known by her stage names, Petite Miss, Evie Bricks, and Big E, is a Utician rapper, actress, model, and reality TV personality. Born and raised in G-block of the Uptin HP, Banks lives most of her adolescent life on the streets after running away from her abusive childhood home. She kept out of too much trouble by finding a rap crew to freestyle with. This street crew is how she was discovered by Royal C.R.N.N and given an opportunity to make something of herself. Banks released 4 studio albums spanning 1996 through 2005. The biggest controversy of her career was not being the drug dealer's side chick, but instead surrounded the fact that she was heavily coached by C.R.N.N and possibly even had him writing her lyrics. Because she was touted as nothing more than a ratchet sex symbol, it was never determined whether or not she deserved respect as an artist.

- **<u>TrampStompers:</u>** It's no surprise that TrampStompers exist on Th'aer as well as the Finding New Haven Earth. The high end shoe company specializes in all things high-heels and has been the picture of cutting edge footwear for nearly a century.

- **<u>Pine daisy:</u>** Th'aerian term for chamomile.

- **<u>Alexander and Joanie:</u>** Alexander Claude McPeters and Joanie Rose Clark were an Utician criminal couple who traveled Middle Utimas during the Great Struggle. They were mostly known for their bank robberies, despite the fact that their preference was robbing small stores, and even funeral homes.

- **<u>The Great Struggle:</u>** the Utician financial depression of 1929, which lasted a decade and devastated families all across Utimas until 1939.

Just have fun with it.

If you have fun writing it, your readers will have fun <u>reading</u> it.

That's kind of the entire point of Lazy Worldbuilding and Pop Culture Creation, having fun writing so that you will have something fun to read once you're done, from cover to cover.

Chapter 6.2 – Exploring History

Depending on the age of your characters, you may find yourself traipsing though the sands of time for your world building research.

If you have a character who is 300 years old, for example, it becomes your responsibility to understand what their perspective would be, and that comes with research. Especially because you most likely have no idea what it's like to be 300 years old, and should flesh out that perspective before actually writing a story from their viewpoint in modern times.

Here's the thing: as an author, you need to <u>embrace</u> the researching process.

Learning more about the world in order to enhance your craft shows that you are living in growth mindset and it will set your work worlds apart from that of more frivolous authors.

Even if you <u>never</u> have to do <u>any</u> research for your story-line, you will find yourself needing to do some mild research to put your glossary together, because a <u>lot</u> of contemporary brands have actually been around for decades.

The brutal truth of the matter is that if you only "write what you know," you're <u>going</u> to run out of stories to tell.

But, if you write what you're <u>interested in</u>, and you're willing to learn more about that topic, you will <u>never</u> experience writer's block again.

Don't limit yourself.

Open doors for yourself instead, so that you can explore things you've never thought about before and expand your perspective.

Become limitless.

Free yourself.

<u>Do research.</u>
Explore the sands of time and see where they take you.
You may just surprise yourself.

<u>Chapter 6.3 – Building Your World, *Beyond* Your Story</u>

Once you've built up a world that you're proud of, and you've published a few books, you could always use all the information you've gathered and brands you've created in places *other than* your story.

Now that you have your World Guide, you could always take a page out of J.K. Rowling's book and put together a history book, or even a reader facing World Guide, and publish that for your super fans.

You could also go the extra step and start spreading brand awareness for the pop culture you've created.

One of my favorite parts of some of the cross over brands on Th'aer and (the former) Horror Hollows is that I get to cross reference the two worlds in the glossary.

Here is an example of one brand located on both planets, from one of the Th'aerian glossaries:

- <u>Pump'n'Gulp:</u> *This is another company with such vast amounts of power that it transcends space and time. However, the signature colors for Pump'n'Gulp in the Finding New Haven universe are purple and blue, while Th'aerian Pump'n'Gulps are green and yellow. The Pump'n'Gulp is a national convenience store chain, oftentimes sprawling in nature and accompanied with the occasional car wash, obligatory casino, and in larger areas, a hotel. Set apart by its green and yellow branding and uniforms, Pump'n'Gulp was founded in 1953 by a young woman with a dream in her heart, a fire in her soul, and an inheritance to invest.

If you're really ambitious, you could pick your most prominent brands and make merch for them.

When it comes to turning your writing empire into an even more powerful source of income, this is a *great* way to create super fans.

You could even create a package deal where readers can buy a signed copy of your book, or a set of books, complete with a T-shirt or two with your home-planet's brands on them to help create a completely immersive experience for your readers.

And this is actually entirely doable, all thanks to the boom of print-on-demand T-shirt companies in the last couple of decades.

There are plenty of resources out there that will help you create your author sit, your mailing list, and show you how to build a print-on-demand platform, but that is far too much information for me to compile here.

However, once you get to the point of having all those pieces in place, now you will have an idea of how to optimize all this work you've put into your craft.

You've created a world, built an entire planet, and crafted your own pop culture... I am sure that your readers would <u>LOVE</u> to wear a T-shirt with one of your home-planet's brands on it.

I know I would!

Thank you for reading <u>Creating Pop Culture!</u>

If you felt this book was helpful to you and your craft, shoot me an email through my website: www.eirianwrites.com[1] so that I can personally send you an exclusive link to join my Writer's Room on Discord.

See you there!

---

1.   https://www.eirianwrites.com/

Don't miss out!

Visit the website below and you can sign up to receive emails whenever E. Naomi Omid publishes a new book. There's no charge and no obligation.

https://books2read.com/r/B-A-JLOJ-CDAXC

BOOKS 2 READ

Connecting independent readers to independent writers.

Did you love *Creating Pop Culture*? Then you should read *All Th'aer (Box Set)*[2] by E. Naomi Omid!

3 Separate Series All Taking Place on 1 World

Welcome to Th'aer, whear East is Wenst. A place that seems very familiar, but is full of surprises and magic.

Faries, mermaids, talking cats, and so much more await inside this four book collection!

Here you will find all of E. Naomi Omid's Th'aerian works, including:

Did You Hear About the Prinz Party - Where it all began... the first story to take place on Th'aer where your favorite

2. https://books2read.com/u/m0oXZA

3. https://books2read.com/u/m0oXZA

Faerie Tales get a modern twist.**Flashbacks & Afterglow** - the zany sequel to <u>Did You Hear About the Prinz Party</u> that explores yet another "Prinz Party" and has an odd <u>12 Dancing Sisters</u> side plot that is sure to thrill you.**PNK KanD Project: Book One - Breakout** - The first installment of the <u>PNK KanD Project</u> book series where PNK KanD begins telling her origin story to the main character of <u>Did You Hear About the Prinz Party</u> (**Including the original music from the book!**)**#SelfishSunday** - the first installment of the <u>Keoni Magnolia Series</u> in which a young woman travels through time to heal her trauma**PLUS** 5 Bonus Keoni Magnolia short stories, poems, and journal entries, previously only published on E. Naomi's website.

Thats <u>4</u> full length books **AND** 1 deluxe EP, all in one place!

So, what're you waiting for?

Isn't it time to go Th'aer?

Read more at https://www.eirianwrites.com/.

Also by E. Naomi Omid

Finding New Haven
Finding New Haven

Keoni Magnolia
#SelfishSunday

PNK KanD Project
Breakout

Standalone
All Th'aer (Box Set)
Creating Pop Culture

Watch for more at https://www.eirianwrites.com/.

About the Author

E. Naomi Omid was born and raised in the Gallatin Valley and is the survivor of teenage relationship abuse. As a result, this cosmic faerie is on a mission to help spread love and light to all who need it.

E. Naomi has innumerable titles across several book series, all within the speculative literature genre. She is also known to publish inspirational self-help books focused on affirmations on the side; and is currently most proud of her PNK KanD Project - an extensive book series with original music to go with each book that is written and performed by the author herself.

This cosmic faerie is a certified life and mindset coach who delights in helping all of the Sugar Plums on the planet discover, heal, and step into their highest state of being, for a better self, and a better world.

Discover all of the things E. Naomi has for what ails you at her homebase: www.eirianwrites.com

Read more at https://www.eirianwrites.com/.

About the Publisher

EirianWrites Studios is a multi-media company specializing in written word as well as audio and visual content.

Founded in 2021, EirianWrites Studio prides itself on innovating the ever changing entertainment industry by providing you with new and exciting experiences, and new ways to fully immerse yourself into what you are reading.

Rep your favorite fictional brands. Head over to the EirianWrites Boutique today!

Read more at https://www.eirianwrites.com.